A CALL FOR
COURAGE

A CALL FOR
COURAGE

———◦◦((◦))◦◦———

BRYAN CURTIS, Editor

RUTLEDGE HILL PRESS™

Nashville, Tennessee

A DIVISION OF THOMAS NELSON, INC.
www.ThomasNelson.com

Published by Rutledge Hill Press,
a division of Thomas Nelson, Inc., P.O. Box 141000,
Nashville, Tennessee 37214.

Photos on pages 21, 57, and 75 courtesy of National Archives. Photos
on pages 39 and 111 courtesy of Library of Congress. Photo on page
93 courtesy of Jimmy Carter Library.

Design by Gore Studio Inc.

Library of Congress Cataloging-in-Publication Data

A call for courage / Bryan Curtis, editor.
    p. cm.
    ISBN 1-40160-002-6
    1. Presidents—United States—Quotations. 2. Courage—Quotations, maxims,
etc. 3. United States—Politics and government—Quotations, maxims, etc. I.
Curtis, Bryan.
    E176.1 .C15 2002
    973'09'9—dc21   2002008629

Printed in the United States of America

02 03 04 05 06 — 5 4 3 2 1

FOR MY SISTER, KELLY SIMS

Preface

———◆———

When people think about the need for courage, images that may come to mind are a soldier going off into battle or a firefighter entering a burning building—and obviously courage is necessary at those times. But even if you never face these hazardous situations, there will be times in your life when courage is needed. This may be when you get behind the wheel of a car for the first time, when you are going on a job interview, or when you must face surgery.

Throughout our history, our presidents have called on Americans to have courage and have praised those who showed it under remarkable circumstances.

Andrew Jackson encouraged a nation not to give in to a lack of confidence when he said, "Never take counsel of your fears." And Franklin D. Roosevelt advised, "When you see a rattlesnake poised to strike you, do not wait until he has struck before you crush him." These messages can be applied to many circumstances in anyone's life—from battling an illness to a business crisis.

Ronald Reagan paid tribute to the brave men and women who lost their lives on the space shuttle *Challenger* when he said, "We will never forget them, nor the last time we saw them—this morning, as they prepared for their journey, and waved good-bye, and 'slipped the surly bonds of earth' to 'touch the face of God.'" With these words, he not only praised the courage of those astronauts, but also called on our nation to honor those heroes while we grieved.

I hope you will find something in this book that will help you bolster your courage—whether it is the courage needed to meet challenges in your personal or professional life, or to make sacrifices for the benefit of others and your nation.

I also hope you take a moment to think about all the heroes who have never taken counsel of their fears—and the great nation we enjoy as a result.

America was not built on fear. America was built on courage, on imagination and an unbeatable determination to do the job at hand.

—HARRY S. TRUMAN

When written in Chinese, the word "crisis" is composed of two characters. One represents danger, and the other represents opportunity.

—JOHN F. KENNEDY

No arsenal or no weapon in the arsenals of the world is so formidable as the will and moral courage of free men and women.

—RONALD REAGAN

Americans, indeed all freemen, remember that in the final choice, a soldier's pack is not so heavy a burden as a prisoner's chains.

—DWIGHT D. EISENHOWER

Stand with anybody that stands right. Stand with him while he is right, and part with him when he goes wrong.

—ABRAHAM LINCOLN

Far better it is to dare mighty things, to win glorious triumphs, even though checkered by failure, than to take rank with those poor spirits who neither enjoy much nor suffer much, because they live in the great twilight that knows neither victory nor defeat.

—THEODORE ROOSEVELT

Never take counsel of your fears.

—ANDREW JACKSON

The people have now gathered their strength. They are moving forward in their might and power—and no force, no combination of forces, no trickery, deceit, or violence, can stop them now. They see before them the hope of the world—a decent, secure, peaceful life for all men everywhere.

—FRANKLIN D. ROOSEVELT

12

The time is now and near at hand which must probably determine whether Americans are to be freemen or slaves; whether they are to have property they can call their own; whether their houses and farms are to be pillaged and destroyed, and themselves consigned to a state of wretchedness from which no human efforts will deliver them. The fate of unborn millions will now depend, under God, on the courage and conduct of this army. Our cruel and unrelenting enemy leaves us no choice but a brave resistance, or the most abject submission. . . . We have, therefore, to resolve to conquer or to die.

—GEORGE WASHINGTON

The only man who never makes a mistake is the man who never does anything.

—THEODORE ROOSEVELT

Let us all stand together as Americans. Let us stand together with all men everywhere who believe in human liberty.

—HARRY S. TRUMAN

Honest conviction is my courage; the Constitution is my guide.

—ANDREW JOHNSON

Th building of such a peace is a bold and solemn purpose. To proclaim it is easy. To serve it will be hard. And to attain it, we must be aware of its full meaning—and ready to pay its full price.

—DWIGHT D. EISENHOWER

I know it's hard when you're up to your armpits in alligators to remember you came here to drain the swamp.

—RONALD REAGAN

Our men on the fighting fronts have already proved that Americans today are just as rugged and just as tough as any of the heroes whose exploits we celebrate on the Fourth of July.

—FRANKLIN D. ROOSEVELT

The tree of liberty must be refreshed from time to time with the blood of patriots and tyrants. It is natural manure.

—THOMAS JEFFERSON

Peace is precious to us. It is the way of life we strive for with all the strength and wisdom we possess. But more precious than peace are freedom and justice. We will fight, if fight we must, to keep our freedom and to prevent justice from being destroyed.

—HARRY S. TRUMAN

Tonight we are a country awakened to danger and called to defend freedom. Our grief has turned to anger, and anger to resolution. Whether we bring our enemies to justice, or bring justice to our enemies, justice will be done. . . . Fellow citizens, we'll meet violence with patient justice—assured of the rightness of our cause, and confident of the victories to come. In all that lies before us, may God grant us wisdom, and may He watch over the United States of America.

—GEORGE W. BUSH

Efforts and courage are not enough without purpose and direction.

—JOHN F. KENNEDY

A vital element in keeping the peace is our military establishment. Our arms must be mighty, ready for instant action, so that no potential aggressor may be tempted to risk his own destruction.

—DWIGHT D. EISENHOWER

I will sacrifice
everything but principle
to procure harmony.

—THOMAS JEFFERSON

One man with courage makes a majority.

—ANDREW JACKSON

It will be a desirable thing to extinguish from the bosom of every member of the community any apprehensions that there are those among his countrymen who wish to deprive them of the liberty for which they valiantly fought and honorably bled.

—JAMES MADISON

This country was founded and built by people with great dreams and the courage to take great risks.

—RONALD REAGAN

Well may the boldest fear and the wisest tremble when incurring responsibilities on which may depend our country's peace and prosperity, and in some degree the hopes and the happiness of the whole human family.

—JAMES K. POLK

A wise and patriotic consistency will never object to the imposition of necessary burdens for useful ends, and true wisdom dictates the resort to such means in order to supply deficiencies in the revenue, rather than to those doubtful expedients which, ultimating in a public debt, serve to embarrass the resources of the country and to lessen its ability to meet any great emergency which may arise.

—JOHN TYLER

For courage—not complacency—is our
need today—leadership—not salesmanship.

—JOHN F. KENNEDY

Love of liberty means the guarding of every
resource that makes freedom possible—
from the sanctity of our families and the
wealth of our soil to the genius of our
scientists.

—DWIGHT D. EISENHOWER

If America wants concessions, she must fight for them. We must purchase our power with our blood.

—JAMES MONROE

We will stand mighty for peace and freedom, and maintain a strong defense against terror and destruction. Our children will sleep free from the threat of nuclear, chemical or biological weapons.

—BILL CLINTON

There is no such a thing as a man being too proud to fight.

—WOODROW WILSON

But we have learned that we can never dig a hole so deep that it would be safe against predatory animals. We have also learned that if we do not pull the fangs of the predatory animals of this world, they will multiply and grow in strength and they will be at our throats once more in a short generation.

—FRANKLIN D. ROOSEVELT

No person was ever honored for what he received. Honor has been the reward for what he gave.

—CALVIN COOLIDGE

Let every American, every lover of liberty, every well-wisher to his posterity, swear by the blood of the Revolution never to violate in the least particular the laws of the country, and never to tolerate their violation by others.

—ABRAHAM LINCOLN

The young men of the country—those who from their age must be its rulers twenty-five years hence—have a peculiar interest in maintaining the national honor. A moment's reflection as to what will be our commanding influence among the nations of the earth in their day, if they are only true to themselves, should inspire them with national pride. All divisions—geographical, political, and religious—can join in this common sentiment.

—ULYSSES S. GRANT

The right of resisting oppression is a natural right.

—Andrew Jackson

———◉———

Victory in this war is the first and greatest goal before us. Victory in the peace is the next. That means striving toward the enlargement of the security of man here and throughout the world—and, finally, striving for the fourth freedom—Freedom from fear.

—Franklin D. Roosevelt

I contend that the strongest of all governments is that which is most free.

—WILLIAM HENRY HARRISON

While I shall sedulously cultivate the relations of peace and amity with one and all, it will be my most imperative duty to see that the honor of the country shall sustain no blemish.

—JOHN TYLER

We have a long way to go, but thanks to the courage, patience, and strength of our people, America is on the mend.

—RONALD REAGAN

My call is to the young in heart, regardless of age—to all who respond to the Scriptural call: "Be strong and of a good courage; be not afraid, neither be thou dismayed."

—JOHN F. KENNEDY

Peace and good will have been, and will hereafter be, cultivated with all, and by the most faithful regard to justice. They have been dictated by a love of peace, of economy, and an earnest desire to save the lives of our fellow-citizens from that destruction and our country from that devastation which are inseparable from war when it finds us unprepared for it.

—JAMES MONROE

This generation of Americans has a rendezvous with destiny.

—FRANKLIN D. ROOSEVELT

Men may die, but the fabrics of our free institutions remain unshaken. No higher or more assuring proof could exist of the strength and permanence of popular government than the fact that though the chosen of the people be struck down, his constitutional successor is peacefully installed without shock or strain except the sorrow which mourns the bereavement.

—CHESTER A. ARTHUR

Take time to deliberate; but when the time for action arrives, stop thinking and go in.

—ANDREW JACKSON

I love to see honest and honorable men at the helm, men who will not bend their politics to their purses nor pursue measures by which they may profit and then profit by their measures.

—THOMAS JEFFERSON

35

The worst fear is the fear of living.

—THEODORE ROOSEVELT

———◦◉◦———

The Americans who went to Europe to die
are a unique breed. Never before have men
crossed the seas to a foreign land to fight for
a cause which they did not pretend was
peculiarly their own, which they knew was
the cause of humanity and mankind. These
Americans gave the greatest of all gifts, the
gift of life and the gift of spirit.

—WOODROW WILSON

When you see a rattlesnake poised to strike you, do not wait until he has struck before you crush him.

—FRANKLIN D. ROOSEVELT

Let every nation know, whether it wishes us well or ill, we shall pay any price, bear any burden, meet any hardship, support any friend, oppose any foe, to assure the survival and success of liberty.

—JOHN F. KENNEDY

We, too, born to freedom, and believing in freedom, are willing to fight to maintain freedom. We and all others who believe as deeply as we do, would rather die on our feet than live on our knees.

—FRANKLIN D. ROOSEVELT

Joseph Stalin, Franklin D. Roosevelt, and Winston Churchill during the Teheran Conference, November 28–December 1, 1943.

I have already transmitted to Congress the report of the naval court of inquiry on the destruction of the battleship *Maine* in the harbor of Havana during the night of the fifteenth of February. The destruction of that noble vessel has filled the national heart with inexpressible horror. Two hundred and fifty-eight brave sailors and marines and two officers of our Navy, reposing in the fancied security of a friendly harbor, have been hurled to death, grief and want brought to their homes and sorrow to the nation.

—WILLIAM McKINLEY

I summon all honest men, all patriotic, all forward-looking men, to my side. God helping me, I will not fail them, if they will but counsel and sustain me!

—WOODROW WILSON

They [veterans of the Allied landing in Normandy] may walk with a little less spring in their step, and the ranks are growing thinner, but let us never forget, when they were young, these men saved the world.

—BILL CLINTON

Let us prove, again, that we are not merely sunshine patriots and summer soldiers. Let us go forward, trusting in the God of Peace, to win the goals we seek.

—HARRY S. TRUMAN

What brought America back? The American people brought us back—with quiet courage and common sense; with undying faith that in this Nation under God the future will be ours, for the future belongs to the free.

—RONALD REAGAN

 A nd so, my fellow Americans: ask not what your country can do for you—ask what you can do for your country.

—JOHN F. KENNEDY

W e feel this moral strength because we know that we are not helpless prisoners of history. We are free men. We shall remain free, never to be proven guilty of the one capital offense against freedom, a lack of staunch faith.

—DWIGHT D. EISENHOWER

43

You cannot win a battle in any arena merely by defending yourself.

—RICHARD M. NIXON

It is the task of our generation, yours and mine. But we build and defend not for our generation alone. We defend the foundations laid down by our fathers. We build a life for generations yet unborn. We defend and we build a way of life, not for America alone, but for all mankind. Ours is a high duty, a noble task.

—FRANKLIN D. ROOSEVELT

The credit belongs to the man who is actually in the arena, whose face is marred by dust and sweat and blood; who strives valiantly; who errs and comes short again and again, who knows the great enthusiasms, the great devotions, and spends himself in a worthy cause; who at best, knows the triumph of high achievement; and who, at the worst, if he fails, at least fails while daring greatly, so that his place shall never be with those cold and timid souls who know neither victory or defeat.

—THEODORE ROOSEVELT

It is impossible, my countrymen, to speak of peace without profound emotion. In thousands of homes in America, in millions of homes around the world, there are vacant chairs. It would be a shameful confession of our unworthiness if it should develop that we have abandoned the hope for which all these men died. Surely civilization is old enough, surely mankind is mature enough so that we ought in our own lifetime to find a way to permanent peace. Abroad, to west and east, are nations whose sons mingled their blood with the blood of our sons on the battlefields. Most of these nations have contributed to our race, to our culture, our knowledge, and our progress. From one of them we derive our very language and from many of them much of the genius of our institutions. Their desire for peace is as deep and sincere as our own.

—HERBERT HOOVER

The boisterous sea of liberty is never without a wave.

—THOMAS JEFFERSON

The Almighty God has blessed our land in many ways. He has given our people stout hearts and strong arms with which to strike mighty blows for freedom and truth. He has given to our country a faith which has become the hope of all peoples in an anguished world.

—FRANKLIN D. ROOSEVELT

The art of war is simple enough. Find out where your enemy is. Get at him as soon as you can. Strike at him as hard as you can, and keep moving on.

—ULYSSES S. GRANT

Let us proudly remember that the members of the Armed Forces give their basic allegiance solely to the United States. Of that fact all of us are certain.

—DWIGHT D. EISENHOWER

Let it be said of us that we, too, did not fail. That we, too, worked together to bring America through difficult times. Let us so conduct ourselves that two centuries from now, another Congress and another President, meeting in this Chamber as we are meeting, will speak of us with pride, saying that we met the test and preserved for them in their day the sacred flame of liberty—this last, best hope of man on Earth.

—RONALD REAGAN

Let us have faith that right makes might.

—ABRAHAM LINCOLN

———◆———

A nation is not worthy to be saved if, in the hour of its fate, it will not gather up all its jewels of manhood and life, and go down into the conflict, however bloody and doubtful, resolved on measureless ruin or complete success.

—JAMES A. GARFIELD

I have always done my duty. I am ready to die. My only regret is for the friends I leave behind.

—Zachary Taylor

The right of self-defense never ceases. It is among the most sacred, and alike necessary to nations and to individuals.

—James Monroe

We are going to have peace, even if we have to fight for it.

—Dwight D. Eisenhower

The individual who refuses to defend his rights when called by his Government, deserves to be a slave, and must be punished as an enemy of his country and friend to her foe.

—Andrew Jackson

Courtesy is as much a mark of a gentleman as courage.

—THEODORE ROOSEVELT

These acts were intended to frighten us, but they have failed. Terrorist acts can shake the foundations of our biggest buildings but cannot touch the foundation of America.

—GEORGE W. BUSH

The men of Normandy had faith that what they were doing was right, faith that they fought for all humanity, faith that a just God would grant them mercy on this beachhead or the next. It was the deep knowledge—and pray God we have not lost it—that there is a profound moral difference between the use of force for liberation and the use of force for conquest.

—RONALD REAGAN

What counts is not necessarily the size of the dog in the fight—it's the size of the fight in the dog.

—DWIGHT D. EISENHOWER

The first duty of law is to keep sound the society it serves.

—WOODROW WILSON

Now the trumpet summons us again—not as a call to bear arms, though arms we need; not as a call to battle, though embattled we are—but a call to bear the burden of a long twilight struggle, year in and year out, "rejoicing in hope, patient in tribulation"—a struggle against the common enemies of man: tyranny, poverty, disease, and war itself.

—JOHN F. KENNEDY

We are face to face with our destiny and we must meet it with a high and resolute courage.

—THEODORE ROOSEVELT

Only if you have been in the deepest valley can you ever know how magnificent it is to be on the highest mountain.

—RICHARD M. NIXON

Indeed, in the old acceptation of the word, virtue included strength and courage, for the clear-sighted men at the dawn of our era knew that the passive virtues could not by themselves avail, that wisdom without courage would sink into mere cunning, and courage without morality into ruthless, lawless, self-destructive ferocity.

—THEODORE ROOSEVELT

Democracy is worth dying for, because it's the most deeply honorable form of government ever devised by man.

—RONALD REAGAN

Confidence . . . thrives on honesty, on honor, on the sacredness of obligations, on faithful protection and on unselfish performance. Without them it cannot live.

—FRANKLIN D. ROOSEVELT

If I am shot at, I want no man to be in the way of the bullet.

—ANDREW JOHNSON

Let those who would die for the flag on the field of battle give a better proof of their patriotism and a higher glory to their country by promoting fraternity and justice.

—BENJAMIN HARRISON

Fighting battles is like courting girls: those who make the most pretensions and are boldest usually win.

—RUTHERFORD B. HAYES

Every citizen owes to the country a vigilant watch and close scrutiny of its public servants and affairs and a reasonable estimate of their fidelity and usefulness.

—GROVER CLEVELAND

We in this Union enter the last decade of the 20th century thankful for our blessings, steadfast in our purpose, aware of our difficulties, and responsive to our duties at home and around the world. For two centuries, America has served the world as an inspiring example of freedom and democracy. For generations, America has led the struggle to preserve and extend the blessings of liberty. And today, in a rapidly changing world, American leadership is indispensable. Americans know that leadership brings burdens and sacrifices. But we also know why the hopes of humanity turn to us. We are Americans; we have a unique responsibility to do the hard work of freedom. And when we do, freedom works.

—GEORGE BUSH

The fight must go on. The cause of civil liberty must not be surrendered at the end of one or even one hundred defeats.

—ABRAHAM LINCOLN

This is a day when all Americans from every walk of life unite in our resolve for justice and peace. . . . America has stood down enemies before, and we will do so this time.

—GEORGE W. BUSH

To maintain peace in the future it is necessary to be prepared for war.

—ULYSSES S. GRANT

The plain people of this country found the courage and the strength, the self-discipline, and the mutual respect to fight and to win, with the help of our allies, under God. I doubt if the tasks of the future are more difficult. But if they are, then I say that our strength and our knowledge and our understanding will be equal to those tasks.

—HARRY S. TRUMAN

The American people are slow to wrath, but when their wrath is once kindled it burns like a consuming flame.

—THEODORE ROOSEVELT

Every citizen should be a soldier. This was the case with the Greeks and Romans, and must be that of every free state.

—THOMAS JEFFERSON

If we meet our responsibilities, I think freedom will conquer. If we fail, if we fail to move ahead, if we fail to develop sufficient military and economic and social strength here in this country, then I think that the tide could begin to run against us, and I don't want historians ten years from now to say, these were the years when the tide ran out for the United States. I want them to say, these were the years when the tide came in, these were the years when the United States started to move again. That's the question before the American People, and only you can decide what you want, what you want this country to be, what you want to do with the future.

—JOHN F. KENNEDY

This hand, to tyrants ever sworn the foe,
For freedom only deals the deadly blow;
Then sheathes in calm repose the vengeful
   blade,
For gentle peace in Freedom's hallowed
   shade.

—JOHN ADAMS

Be honest, and remember that honesty counts for nothing unless back of it lie courage and efficiency.

—THEODORE ROOSEVELT

Our men have fought with indescribable and unforgettable gallantry under most difficult conditions, and our German enemies have sustained considerable losses while failing to obtain their objectives.

—FRANKLIN D. ROOSEVELT

71

Actions speak louder than words.

—THEODORE ROOSEVELT

They came here—the exile and the stranger, brave but frightened—to find a place where a man could be his own man. They made a covenant with this land. Conceived in justice, written in liberty, bound in union, it was meant one day to inspire the hopes of all mankind; and it binds us still. If we keep its terms, we shall flourish.

—LYNDON B. JOHNSON

Think of your forefathers! Think of your posterity.

—JOHN ADAMS

Today we affirm a new commitment to live out our nation's promise through civility, courage, compassion and character.

—GEORGE W. BUSH

A brave man is a man who dares to look the Devil in the face and tell him he is a Devil.

—JAMES A. GARFIELD

The long roll call, all the G.I. Joes and Janes, all the ones who fought faithfully for freedom, who hit the ground and sucked the dust and knew their share of horror. This may seem frivolous, and I don't mean it so, but it's moving to me how the world saw them. The world saw not only their special valor but their special style: their rambunctious, optimistic bravery, their do-or-die unity unhampered by class or race or region. What a group we've put forth, for generations now, from the ones who wrote "Kilroy was here" on the walls of the German stalags to those who left signs in the Iraqi desert that said, "I saw Elvis." What a group of kids we've sent out into the world.

—GEORGE BUSH

The unforgivable crime is soft hitting. Do not hit at all if it can be avoided; but never hit softly.

—THEODORE ROOSEVELT

———⊷◉⊶———

Peace is the highest aspiration of the American people. We will negotiate for it, sacrifice for it; we will never surrender for it, now or ever.

—RONALD REAGAN

A pound of pluck is worth a ton of luck.

—JAMES A. GARFIELD

From a just responsibility I will never shrink, calculating with confidence that in my best efforts to promote the public welfare my motives will always be duly appreciated and my conduct be viewed with that candor and indulgence which I have experienced in other stations.

—JAMES MONROE

Let your heart feel for the affliction and distress of everyone.

—GEORGE WASHINGTON

The American people will never stop to reckon the cost of redeeming civilization. They know there never can be any economic justification for failing to save freedom.

—FRANKLIN D. ROOSEVELT

Our objectives are clear. Our forces are strong, and our cause is right.

—BILL CLINTON

In the long history of the world, only a few generations have been granted the role of defending freedom in its hour of maximum danger. . . . The energy, the faith, the devotion which we bring to this endeavor will light our country and all who serve it, and the glow from that fire can truly light the world.

—JOHN F. KENNEDY

In reading the lives of great men, I found that the first victory they won was over themselves . . . self-discipline with all of them came first. Men make history and not the other way around. In periods where there is no leadership, society stands still. Progress occurs when courageous, skillful leaders seize the opportunity to change things for the better.

—HARRY S. TRUMAN

What great crises teach all men whom the example and counsel of the brave inspire is the lesson: Fear not, view all the tasks of life as sacred, have faith in the triumph of the ideal, give daily all that you have to give, be loyal and rejoice whenever you find yourselves part of a great ideal enterprise. You, at this moment, have the honor to belong to a generation whose lips are touched by fire. You live in a land that now enjoys the blessings of peace. But let nothing human be wholly alien to you. The human race now passes through one of its great crises. New ideas, new issues—a new call for men to carry on the work of righteousness, of charity, of courage, of patience, and of loyalty. . . . However memory bring back this moment to your minds, let it be able to say to you: That was a great moment. It was the beginning of a new era. . . . This world in its crisis called for volunteers, for men of faith in life, of patience in service, of charity and of insight. I responded to the call however I could. I volunteered to give myself to my Master— the cause of humane and brave living. I studied, I loved, I labored, unsparingly and hopefully, to be worthy of my generation.

—FRANKLIN D. ROOSEVELT

Pessimism never won any battle.

—DWIGHT D. EISENHOWER

The ground of liberty is to be gained by inches, and we must be contented to secure what we can get from time to time and eternally press forward for what is yet to get. It takes time to persuade men to do even what is for their own good.

—THOMAS JEFFERSON

As long as the United States of America is determined and strong, this will not be an age of terror. This will be an age of liberty here and across the world.

—GEORGE W. BUSH

Always bear in mind that your own resolution to succeed is more important than any other one thing.

—ABRAHAM LINCOLN

The path we have chosen for the present is full of hazards, as all paths are—but it is the one most consistent with our character and courage as a nation and our commitments around the world. The cost of freedom is always high—and Americans have always paid it. And one path we shall never choose, and that is the path of surrender or submission.

—JOHN F. KENNEDY

No one need think that the world can be ruled without blood. The civil sword shall and must be red and bloody.

—ANDREW JACKSON

Of course the all-important thing to keep in mind is that if we have not both strength and virtue we shall fail.

—THEODORE ROOSEVELT

The finest steel has to go through the hottest fire.

—RICHARD M. NIXON

When even one American—who has done nothing wrong—is forced by fear to shut his mind and close his mouth—then all Americans are in peril.

—HARRY S. TRUMAN

The man who can look upon a crisis without being willing to offer himself upon the altar of his country is not fit for public trust.

—MILLARD FILLMORE

Always remember that an armed and trained militia is the firmest bulwark of republics—that without standing armies their liberty can never be in danger, nor with large ones safe.

—JAMES MADISON

89

History does not long entrust the care of freedom to the weak or the timid.

—DWIGHT D. EISENHOWER

Discipline is the soul of an army. It makes small numbers formidable, procures success to the weak, and esteem to all.

—GEORGE WASHINGTON

The overwhelming majority of our people have met the demands of this war with magnificent courage and understanding. They have accepted inconveniences; they have accepted hardships; they have accepted tragic sacrifices. And they are ready and eager to make whatever further contributions are needed to win the war as quickly as possible—if only they are given the chance to know what is required of them.

—FRANKLIN D. ROOSEVELT

We have no desire to be the world's policeman. But America does want to be the world's peacemaker.

—JIMMY CARTER

Menachem Begin, Jimmy Carter, and Anwar Sadat at Camp David, September 7, 1978.

Justice and goodwill will outlast passion.

—JAMES A. GARFIELD

A man who is good enough to shed his blood for his country is good enough to be given a square deal, because he is entitled to no more and should receive no less.

—THEODORE ROOSEVELT

The greatest honor history can bestow is that of peacemaker.

—RICHARD M. NIXON

We will never forget them [the men and women on the space shuttle *Challenger*], nor the last time we saw them—this morning, as they prepared for their journey, and waved good-bye, and "slipped the surly bonds of earth" to "touch the face of God."

—RONALD REAGAN

First in importance in the American scene has been the inspiring proof of the great qualities of our fighting men. They have demonstrated these qualities in adversity as well as in victory. As long as our flag flies over this Capitol, Americans will honor the soldiers, sailors, and marines who fought our first battles of this war against overwhelming odds—the heroes, living and dead, of Wake and Bataan and Guadalcanal, of the Java Sea and Midway and the North Atlantic convoys. Their unconquerable spirit will live forever.

—FRANKLIN D. ROOSEVELT

If our country does not lead the cause for freedom, it will not be led.

—George W. Bush

———◦◉◦———

When you are in any contest, you should work as if there were to the very last minute—a chance to lose it. This is battle, this is politics, this is anything.

—Dwight D. Eisenhower

There is no indispensable man.

—Woodrow Wilson

Adhere to your purpose and you will soon feel as well as you ever did. On the contrary, if you falter, and give up, you will lose the power to keep any resolution, and will regret it all your life. Take the advice of a friend . . . and stick to your purpose.

—Abraham Lincoln

Actions are the seeds of fate. Deeds grow into destiny.

—HARRY S. TRUMAN

Any man worth his salt will stick up for what he believes right, but it takes a slightly better man to acknowledge instantly and without reservation that he is in error.

—ANDREW JACKSON

Service is the supreme commitment of life.

—WARREN G. HARDING

The courage of life is often a less dramatic spectacle than the courage of a final moment; but is no less a magnificent mixture of triumph and tragedy.

—JOHN F. KENNEDY

There can be no real peace while one American is dying some place in the world [Vietnam] for the rest of us. We are at war with the most dangerous enemy that has ever faced mankind in his long climb from the swamp to the stars, and it has been said if we lost that war, and in doing so lost this way of freedom of ours, history will record with the greatest astonishment that those who had the most to lose did the least to prevent its happening. . . . If we lose freedom here, there is no place to escape to. This is the last stand on Earth.

—RONALD REAGAN

We dare not forget today that we are the heirs of that first revolution. Let the word go forth from this time and place, to friend and foe alike, that the torch has been passed to a new generation of Americans—born in this century, tempered by war, disciplined by a hard and bitter peace, proud of our ancient heritage—and unwilling to witness or permit the slow undoing of those human rights to which this Nation has always been committed, and to which we are committed today at home and around the world.

—JOHN F. KENNEDY

There is nothing so likely to produce peace as to be well prepared to meet the enemy.

—GEORGE WASHINGTON

You must remember, my fellow citizens, that eternal vigilance by the people is the price of liberty, and that you must pay the price if you wish to secure the blessing.

—ANDREW JACKSON

The nation's honor is dearer than the nation's comfort; yes, than the nation's life itself.

—WOODROW WILSON

Resolute in our determination to respect the rights of others, and to command respect for the rights of ourselves, we must keep ourselves adequately strong in self-defense.

—FRANKLIN D. ROOSEVELT

We have every right to dream heroic dreams. Those who say that we're in a time when there are no heroes, they just don't know where to look.

—RONALD REAGAN

If it be the pleasure of Heaven that my country shall require the poor offering of my life, the victim shall be ready. . . . But while I do live, let me have a country, or at least the hope of a country, and that a free country.

—JOHN ADAMS

We in our turn have an assured confidence that we shall be able to leave this heritage unwasted and enlarged to our children and our children's children. To do so we must show, not merely in great crises, but in the everyday affairs of life, the qualities of practical intelligence, of courage, of hardihood, and endurance, and above all the power of devotion to a lofty ideal, which made great the men who founded this Republic in the days of Washington, which made great the men who preserved this Republic in the days of Abraham Lincoln.

—THEODORE ROOSEVELT

Let us never negotiate out of fear. But let us never fear to negotiate.

—JOHN F. KENNEDY

It is the duty of a citizen not only to observe the law, but to let it be known that he is opposed to its violation.

—CALVIN COOLIDGE

I cannot speak to you tonight about Vietnam without paying a very personal tribute to the men who have carried the battle out there for all of us. I have been honored to be their Commander in Chief. The Nation owes them its unstinting support while the battle continues—and its enduring gratitude when their service is done.

—LYNDON B. JOHNSON

Dollars and guns are no substitutes for brains and will power.

—DWIGHT D. EISENHOWER

Our Government springs from and was made for the people—not the people for the Government. To them it owes allegiance; from them it must derive its courage, strength, and wisdom.

—ANDREW JOHNSON

Courage and perseverance have a magical talisman, before which difficulties disappear and obstacles vanish into air.

—JOHN QUINCY ADAMS

Speak softly and carry a big stick; you will go far.

—THEODORE ROOSEVELT

The ultimate determinant in the struggle now going on for the world will not be bombs and rockets but a test of wills and ideas—a trial of spiritual resolve; the values we hold, the beliefs we cherish and the ideas to which we are dedicated.

—RONALD REAGAN

As we meet here today, American soldiers are fighting a bitter campaign in Korea. We pay tribute to their courage, devotion, and gallantry. Our men are fighting, alongside their United Nations allies, because they know, as we do, that the aggression in Korea is part of the attempt of the Russian Communist dictatorship to take over the world, step by step. Our men are fighting a long way from home, but they are fighting for our lives and our liberties. They are fighting to protect our right to meet here today—our right to govern ourselves as a free nation.

—HARRY S. TRUMAN

Preparation for war is constant stimulus to suspicion and ill will.

—JAMES MONROE

But I do not think that any of us Americans can be content with mere survival. Sacrifices that we and our allies are making impose upon us all a sacred obligation to see to it that out of this war we and our children will gain something better than mere survival.

—FRANKLIN D. ROOSEVELT

Nothing is more harmful to the service, than the neglect of discipline; for that discipline, more than numbers, gives one army superiority over another.

—GEORGE WASHINGTON

America demands and deserves big things from us—and nothing big ever came from being small.

—BILL CLINTON

While we speak of the preparation of the nation to make sure of her security and her effective power, we must not fall into the patent error of supposing that her real strength comes from armaments and mere safeguards of written law. It comes, of course, from her people, their energy, their success in their undertakings, their free opportunity to use the natural resources of our great homeland and of the lands outside our continental borders which look to us for protection, for encouragement, and for assistance in their development; from the organization and freedom of our economic life.

—WOODROW WILSON

This is a time for courage, not for grumbling and mumbling.

—HARRY S. TRUMAN

This is not, however, just America's fight. And what is at stake is not just America's freedom. This is the world's fight. This is civilization's fight. This is the fight of all who believe in progress and pluralism, tolerance and freedom.

—GEORGE W. BUSH

For of those to whom much is given, much is required. And when at some future date the high court of history sits in judgment on each one of us—recording whether in our brief span of service we fulfilled our responsibilities to the state—our success or failure, in whatever office we may hold, will be measured by the answers to four questions. First, were we truly men of courage—with the courage to stand up to one's enemies—and the courage to stand up, when necessary, to one's associates—the courage to resist public pressure, as well as private greed? Secondly, were we truly men of judgment—with perceptive judgment of the future as well as the past—of our own mistakes as well as the mistakes of others—with enough wisdom to know that we did not know, and enough candor to admit it? Third, were we truly men of integrity—men who never ran out on either the principles in which they believed or the people who believed in them—men who believed in us—men whom neither financial gain nor political ambition could ever divert from the fulfillment of our sacred trust? Finally, were we truly men of dedication—with an honor mortgaged to no single individual or group, and compromised by no private obligation or aim, but devoted solely to serving the public good and the national interest?

—JOHN F. KENNEDY

The ablest man I ever met is the man you think you are.

—FRANKLIN D. ROOSEVELT

Carry the battle to them. Don't let them bring it to you. Put them on the defensive and don't ever apologize for anything.

—HARRY S. TRUMAN

I'd rather give my life than be afraid to give it.

—LYNDON B. JOHNSON

His [Jackie Robinson's] courage, his sense of brotherhood, and his brilliance on the playing field brought a new human dimension not only to the game of baseball but to every area of American life where black and white people work side by side.

—RICHARD M. NIXON

To the victors belong the spoils.

—Andrew Jackson

———◆———

Our goal is not the victory of might, but the vindication of right—not peace at the expense of freedom, but both peace and freedom, here in this hemisphere, and, we hope, around the world. God willing, that goal will be achieved.

—John F. Kennedy

What we all thank God for with deepest gratitude is that our men went in force into the line of battle just at the critical moment when the whole fate of the whole world seemed to hang in the balance and threw their fresh strength into the ranks of freedom in time to turn the whole tide and sweep the fateful struggle, turn it once and for all, so that thenceforth it was back, back, back for their enemies, always back, never again forward! After that it was only a scant four months before the commanders of the Central Empires knew themselves beaten; and now their very empires are in liquidation!

—WOODROW WILSON

123

God gave us Lincoln and liberty. Let's fight for both.

—Ulysses S. Grant

To stand upon ramparts and die for our principles is heroic, but to sally forth to battle and win for our principles is something more than heroic.

—Franklin D. Roosevelt

A man is not finished when he is defeated. He is finished when he quits.

—RICHARD M. NIXON

We've defeated freedom's enemies before, and we will defeat them again. We have refused to live in a state of panic or in a state of denial. There is a difference between being alert and being intimidated and this great nation will never be intimidated.

—GEORGE W. BUSH

125

We will always remember. We will always be proud. We will always be prepared, so we may always be free.

—RONALD REAGAN

We can not overestimate the fervent love of liberty, the intelligent courage, and the sum of common sense with which our fathers made the great experiment of self-government.

—JAMES A. GARFIELD

126

I have a deep and abiding faith in the destiny of free men. With strength and courage, we shall, someday, overcome.

—HARRY S. TRUMAN

The stories of past courage . . . can teach, they can offer hope, they can provide inspiration. But they cannot supply courage itself. For this each man must look into his own soul.

—JOHN F. KENNEDY

PRESIDENTIAL TERMS

1.	George Washington	1789–1797	23.	Benjamin Harrison	1889–1893
2.	John Adams	1797–1801	24.	Grover Cleveland	1893–1897
3.	Thomas Jefferson	1801–1809	25.	William McKinley	1897–1901
4.	James Madison	1809–1817	26.	Theodore Roosevelt	1901–1909
5.	James Monroe	1817–1825	27.	William H. Taft	1909–1913
6.	John Quincy Adams	1825–1829	28.	Woodrow Wilson	1913–1921
7.	Andrew Jackson	1829–1837	29.	Warren G. Harding	1921–1923
8.	Martin Van Buren	1837–1841	30.	Calvin Coolidge	1923–1929
9.	William Henry Harrison	1841	31.	Herbert Hoover	1929–1933
10.	John Tyler	1841–1845	32.	Franklin D. Roosevelt	1933–1945
11.	James K. Polk	1845–1849	33.	Harry S. Truman	1945–1953
12.	Zachary Taylor	1849–1850	34.	Dwight D. Eisenhower	1953–1961
13.	Millard Fillmore	1850–1853	35.	John F. Kennedy	1961–1963
14.	Franklin Pierce	1853–1857	36.	Lyndon B. Johnson	1963–1969
15.	James Buchanan	1857–1861	37.	Richard M. Nixon	1969–1974
16.	Abraham Lincoln	1861–1865	38.	Gerald Ford	1974–1977
17.	Andrew Johnson	1865–1869	39.	Jimmy Carter	1977–1981
18.	Ulysses S. Grant	1869–1877	40.	Ronald Reagan	1981–1989
19.	Rutherford B. Hayes	1877–1881	41.	George Bush	1989–1993
20.	James A. Garfield	1881	42.	Bill Clinton	1993–2001
21.	Chester A. Arthur	1881–1885	43.	George W. Bush	2001–
22.	Grover Cleveland	1885–1889